A gift for

Cristina

from

Shirley

on this date

2008

Warm

and Fuzzy Thoughts

A Little Book of Inspiration

from Florida

KAREN NABOZNY

Book design and illustration by Carol Tornatore

SEASIDE PUBLISHING
Palm Harbor, Florida

Printed in the China

$\mathscr{S}$unshine Words
for a Sunshine Day
in Florida

When You're Down, Pick Me Up,
Your Little Book of Warm
and Fuzzy Thoughts

GOOD MORNING

SUNSHINE!

*I*mprove

your thinking,

improve

your life!

TAKE THE HIGH ROAD

IT LEADS TO HIGH PLACES!

Baby Jakob

$\mathcal{V}$isiting some friends we hadn't seen for a few months, the dad looked at our three-year-old grandson and said, "Jakob, you've really grown."

And Jakob looked at him in ernest and said, "I told you I would!"

*E*very day is a gift,

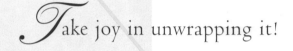

Take joy in unwrapping it!

*O*ur mind
is a battlefield
between
good thoughts
and
bad thoughts.

The Winner

is the one

you feed the most.

Success.....

. . . . is not

the absence

of failure!

Little Kaili

*M*y daughter and I took an afternoon ride to a nearby town to find an address we were looking for.

My little grandaughter, Kaili, was only three then, and she came along for the ride.

I had the map open in front of me and after about ten trips back and forth between the same few blocks, we began to get frustrated.

Kaili asked, What's wrong?"

So I explained. The street we were searching for was right there on the map but we couldn't find it.

"Why not?" She asked.

So I began to explain when all of a sudden she said in a loud, very sure of herself voice,

"Just give me the map!"

VICTORY IS JUST AROUND THE CORNER.

Greatness

is

always

camouflaged

in

the

disguise

of

Children.

FAITH MOVES MOUNTAINS!

"*I*N THY PRESENCE
IS FULLNESS OF JOY;
AT THY RIGHT HAND
THERE ARE PLEASURES
FOR EVERMORE."

[Psalm 16:11]
King James Version of the Bible

NOTHING IS EVER
AS HARD

AS IT FIRST APPEARS.

PLAN YOUR TRIPS

BUT DON'T BE AFRAID OF SPONTANEOUS SIDE TRIPS. SOMETIMES THEY'RE THE MOST FUN!

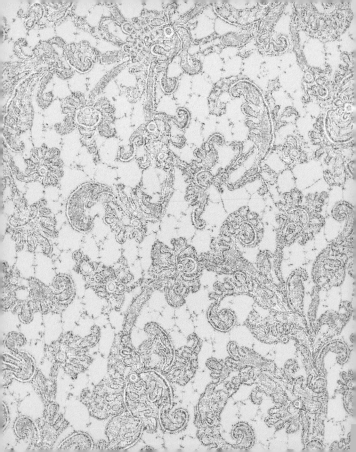

$\mathcal{F}$orgiveness

is for

the Forgiver . . .

One day my friend came over
to visit after returning home from a
week's vacation. We had much to catch
up on, so I made us both a cup of hot tea
and we sat at the table to talk.

After a few minutes, my husband
walked in and wanted to join in the tea
and conversation.

"Honey, where are the cups," He
asked.

"In the left cupboard," I said."

A minute later, "Where're the tea bags?"

"On the counter," I answered.

Then, "How do I make this cup of tea?" He asks.

Finally, out of frustration at being interrupted so often I said, "Oh, just put a tea bag in your mouth and drink some hot water!"

✳ ✳ ✳

The only way to erase
unkindness is with kindness, so
don't lose your eraser!

*P*raise is just like garlic,

In a good salad, a little

goes a long way!

I LOVE YOU
NOT ONLY FOR
WHAT YOU ARE . . .

BUT FOR WHAT I AM
WHEN I AM WITH
YOU.

*O*ne good reason for
not worrying, is that
you won't feel like a
fool when things
turn out alright!

COURAGE IS FEAR THAT

HAS SAID ITS PRAYERS

Faith is needed all the way
Faith to toil and Faith to pray

Faith to learn and Faith to teach
Faith to practice, Faith to preach

Faith to start each day anew
Faith to do our duty too

Faith to help the weak along
Faith to bear in patience, wrong

Faith to smile, though sad within
Faith to conquer every sin

Faith to ask Him for His care
While we earthly trials bear

Faith to smother every sigh
Faith to live and Faith to die.

Little Things

It's just the little homey things,
The unobtrusive, friendly things,
The won't you let me help you things,
That make the pathway light.

And it's just the jolly, joking things,
The laugh with me it's funny things,
The never mind the trouble things,
That make our world seem bright.

For all the countless famous things,
The wondrous record breaking things,
Those never can be equaled things,
That all the papers cite.

Can't match the little human things,
The just because I like you things,
Those oh, it's simply nothing things,
That make us happy quite.

So here's to all the little things,
The everyday encountered things,
The smile and face your trouble things,
Trust God to put it right.

The done and then forgotten things,
The can't you see I love you things,
The hearty I am with you things,
That make life worth the fight.

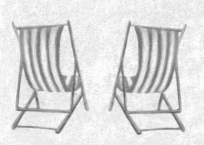

To live above with
saints we love,
Oh, that will be such glory.

To live below with saints
we know,
Well, that's a different story!

WHEN NOBODY DISAGREES
WITH YOU,
YOU CAN ASSURE YOURSELF
THAT YOU ARE
EXCEPTIONALLY BRILLIANT,

OR ELSE YOU'RE THE BOSS.

*Y*ou might as well laugh about it!

I walked into my doctor's new office admiring the decorating. Looking at one of the walls I thought, *What a beautiful aquarium he had in.* After a few seconds Nemo started talking, and I realized it was a high-definition TV mounted on the wall!

We were sightseeing in Florida and happened to be touring an old mansion. The master bedroom was so beautifully furnished we were very surprised to see a sign on the bed and the draperies saying: "Wash your hands immediately after touching."

So we kept our distance but were curious about this warning. When we were leaving, we asked the guard if those fabrics had been treated with some chemical that would be harmful if you touched it.

He said, "No ma'am, grinning, there's no chemicals on them. We just never had any luck with the "Do not touch signs."

He Loves Me

When he came into my life,
    I thought,
"Does he really like me?"

As time went by I found him down
on one knee.
"Yes," I said as we began to dream.
Then all of a sudden, a baby we see.

Now time keeps on flying,
    the babies count three.
Our life is a whirlwind and he really loves me.

By his side I remain, for no others I see
can move all the mountains and still stir
something in me.

So our babies have grown, life's different from then, but the love is much deeper and he's also my friend.

Someone to rely on through thick and through thin
I dare believe forever because I'm with him.

When time ends on earth, together we'll be, holding hands and still dreaming,
It's love can't you see.

He's always amazing, ambitious and free, and I know with no doubt he will always love me.

— *Karen Nabozny*

A Poem for My Mom on Mother's Day

You are so sweet
You are so true
My thoughts are warm
When I think of you.

So caring and loving
Gentle and kind
An angel from above
Simply divine.

Unselfish and pure
Sacrificial and wise
Like a soft summer breeze
Or a morning sunrise.

You bring joy to those around you
Wherever you may go
And when you are away
All I do is miss you so!

You are the heart of our family
You bind us together
You're there when we need you
Through any kind of weather.

You are a special mom
No one else will do
I was blessed from the beginning
Because I have you!

— Nicki Fuller

Granddaughter

Delicate as a dew drop rose,
Fragile as a china cup,
So lovely her arrival
So sweetly we met

Her breath is like the butterfly
Floating on the breeze
The essence of an angel
Is what she leaves.

The touch of innocence and delicate delight
Brings scenes of motherhood long gone
and scents remembered in the nights